W9-AXU-463

Sports Idols™

DANICA PATRICK

Jason Glaser

PowerKiDS press

New York

DISCARD

MEDIA CENTER

For my daughter, Emily, who wants everything higher, faster, scarier, and (most of all) AGAIN

Published in 2008 by The Rosen Publishing Group, Inc.
29 East 21st Street, New York, NY 10010

Copyright © 2008 by The Rosen Publishing Group, Inc.

All rights reserved. No part of this book may be reproduced in any form without permission in writing from the publisher, except by a reviewer.

First Edition

Editor: Amelie von Zumbusch
Book Design: Julio Gil
Photo Researcher: Nicole Pristash

Photo Credits: Cover, pp. 5, 7, 11, 13, 15, 17, 19, 21 © Getty Images; p. 9 Shutterstock.com.

Library of Congress Cataloging-in-Publication Data

Glaser, Jason.
  Danica Patrick / Jason Glaser. — 1st ed.
     p. cm. — (Sports idols)
  Includes index.
  ISBN 978-1-4042-4180-0 (lib. bdg.)
  1. Patrick, Danica, 1982– —Juvenile literature. 2. Automobile racing drivers—United States—Biography—Juvenile literature. 3. Women automobile racing drivers—United States—Biography—Juvenile literature. I. Title.
  GV1032.P38G53 2008
  796.72092—dc22
  [B]
                                                    2007026860

Manufactured in the United States of America

Contents

As a girl, Danica Patrick had the same dream over and over. In Danica's dream, animals with sharp claws were chasing her. One night she dreamed she was moving too fast for them to catch her. Danica fell in love with the idea of **speeding** away from everyone.

Today Danica Patrick races cars that go faster than 200 miles per hour (322 km/h). She drives open-top cars with wheels that are set far apart. These cars move fast and close to the ground. As Patrick drives, she still loves to feel like she is pulling away from roaring monsters behind her.

Danica Patrick, shown here, takes part in many races each year. She races with a group called the IRL, or Indy Racing League.

Going for Go-Karts

Danica was born on March 25, 1982, in Beloit, Wisconsin, but she grew up in Roscoe, Illinois. When Danica was 10, her sister Brooke wanted a go-kart. Brooke and Danica's parents were proud that Brooke wanted to race. Danica's father, T. J. Patrick, had raced a little and talked about it often. The Patricks decided to get go-karts for both Brooke and Danica.

Brooke did not race go-karts for very long, but Danica did. By the age of 12, Danica was winning WKA, or World Karting **Association**, races. At 14, Danica won 39 of the 49 WKA races she entered.

Danica Patrick's parents are big racing fans. Here Danica and her mother, Bev, watch the other racers at the 2006 Milwaukee Mile.

One of Danica's racing teachers was Lyn St. James. St. James was a **professional** race-car driver. She had a racing school for women. St. James knew Danica had talent. She helped send Danica to England to race from 1998 to 2001.

In England, Danica trained hard. She was the only girl, and the other racers often left her out. She had problems getting help with her car. It took Danica years to get a car she liked. With this car, she placed second at the Formula Ford Festival. This was the best any American or woman had ever placed in that race.

In England, Patrick raced mostly Formula Ford cars. Formula Ford cars are low, simple cars with one seat. These cars have big wheels, which are tied to the car with thin bars.

Patrick's driving caught the eye of Bob Rahal. Rahal was the owner of a professional racing team. He wanted to pay Patrick to race in the United States. Rahal entered Patrick in a 10-lap race for **charity**. Patrick took first place and was the first woman to win that race.

The rest of Patrick's early professional years did not go as well. Rahal and Patrick planned to use a kind of car made by BMW. Just before Patrick's first race, new rules kept her from racing in that kind of car. After that Patrick could drive only in small races for a while.

In July 2002, Patrick raced in the Barber Dodge Pro Series, in Vancouver, Canada. She did well and finished in fourth place.

Reaching the Podium

In 2003, a company asked Patrick if it could sponsor her. Sponsors help pay for a car and the people to keep that car working. Rahal and Patrick said yes, and Patrick began racing in the Toyota Atlantic **Series**.

Patrick took third place in her first race. The top three winners stand on a **podium** after the race. Patrick was the first woman to "win a podium" in the Atlantic Series. Later that year, she won second place and made the podium again. In 2004, Patrick made the podium three more times. She also had the third-most points that year.

Patrick worked closely with team owner Bobby Rahal. Here they are chatting before the start of a big race.

The Indianapolis 500

Every open-top race-car driver dreams of racing in the Indianapolis 500. The Indy 500 is the biggest race in the IRL, or Indy Racing **League**. Patrick's driving in the Atlantic Series showed she was ready to start IRL racing.

On May 29, 2005, Patrick became the first woman to lead the Indianapolis 500. Millions of people clapped as they watched her on television. Patrick was in front with six laps left when her car got low on gas. She had to slow down and finished fourth. Patrick's driving still allowed her to win **Rookie** of the Year.

Fans all over the United States watched Patrick lead the Indy 500. She drove
car number 16, the front car in this picture!

A New Team

Many people thought Patrick might win her first race in 2006. However, Rahal wanted to have changes made to Patrick's car. She had trouble driving the car after these changes and never made the podium in 2006. In her return to the Indy 500, Patrick finished in eighth place.

At the end of the season, Patrick left her old team. She joined a team called Andretti Green Racing in 2007. This team was a **rival** of Rahal's team. Changing teams was a hard decision for Patrick to make. However, she felt she needed to join the Andretti team to win.

When she joined Andretti Green, Patrick started driving car number 7.
Here she is with her crew, or the team that works on her car.

SOUTHWEST SCHOOL
MEDIA CENTER

Patrick has made a big mark on racing. Because of her, more people have started watching racing. More girls have started kart racing. More women are finding sponsors and chances to race, too. Patrick is proud to help other women in racing. However, she does not want people to think of her as a woman driver. She just wants to be another driver.

Patrick is also happy to use her **fame** to help people. After the 2005 Indy 500, she gave a part of her car to a charity called Best Buddies Indiana. They sold the $5,000 part for $42,650.11!

Patrick enjoys helping others. In 2006, she visited Camp Heartland, a group that helps children who have the illness HIV/AIDS.

After she came home from England in 2001, Patrick hurt herself doing **yoga**. Rahal asked Patrick to see a **physical therapist** named Paul Hospenthal. Hospenthal and Patrick fell in love as he treated her pain. They married in 2005 and live in Phoenix, Arizona.

Patrick has many ways to slow down off the track. She and her husband like to exercise and eat good food. Patrick also likes watching funny movies and television shows. She loves shopping for new clothes and dressing up in something prettier than a **tracksuit**.

Hospenthal and Patrick dressed up to go to the ESPY Awards. The ESPYs honor the year's best sports players.

Around the Next Turn

As all race-car drivers do, Danica Patrick wants to win. Most racers take around 33 tries to win their first race. The 2007 Indianapolis 500 was Patrick's 35th chance at a win. However, she was in eighth place when the race ended early because of rain.

Good racers know they must make all the right moves to win. Though Patrick did not win the 2007 Indy 500, one of her Andretti Green teammates did. With luck, belonging to a winning team will help Patrick pass under many checkered flags of her own.

Glossary

association (uh-soh-see-AY-shun) A group of people working together for a purpose.

charity (CHER-uh-tee) A group that gives help to the needy.

fame (FAYM) Being very well known.

league (LEEG) People, groups, or countries that work together.

physical therapist (FIH-zih-kul THEHR-uh-pist) A person who helps other people by working with their bodies.

podium (POH-dee-um) A raised stage.

professional (pruh-FESH-nul) Someone who is paid for what he or she does.

rival (RY-vul) Someone who tries to beat someone else at something.

rookie (RU-kee) A new professional racer or player.

series (SIR-eez) A group of races.

speeding (SPEED-ing) Moving very fast.

tracksuit (TRAK-soot) A set of clothes that people wear to exercise or to play a sport.

yoga (YOH-guh) A method of exercising and thinking deeply.

Web Sites

Due to the changing nature of Internet links, PowerKids Press has developed an online list of Web sites related to the subject of this book. This site is updated regularly. Please use this link to access the list:
www.powerkidslinks.com/sidol/danica/